The property Investor's Finance Manifesto

ENGLAND & WALES EDITION

Michael Webb

MICHAEL WEBB

MICHAEL WEBB

Copyright © 2019 Michael Webb
All rights reserved.

ISBN: 9781095982488

Editor's Note

This book is intended for information purposes only. Nothing within should be deemed as advice. If you need mortgage advice you should seek it out from a whole of market broker who can tailor solutions to your specific needs.

Index

About the Author…………………………………………........	1
Buy to let regulations………………………………………	4
Types of Buy to let Mortgages…………………………..	11
Limited Company Buy to let…………. ………………..	13
The Angel Investor………………………………………….	23
Attracting Angel Investors……………………………..	25
HMO Mortgages…………………………………………….	29
Rental Calculations……..…………………………………	35
How to Raise 100% Finance……………………………..	39
Air BNB & Holiday lets…………………………………..	43
Different Types of Mortgage Brokers/Advisor……….	47
Surveys and Mortgage Valuation……………………….	59
Ways to repay your Mortgage………………………….	69
Documents Required…………………………………….	73
Types of Mortgage Products…………………………..	77
First time buyer – Buying to let……………………….	87
Types of Mortgage insurance………………………….	93
Reviewing you insurances………………………….......	103
Types of adverse credit…………………………………	109
Improving your credit file………………………………	113
Common investor mistakes…………………………….	117
Bridging finance………………………………………….	121
Flipping Profit…………………………………………….	129
GLOSSARY of terms…………………………………….	134

About the Author

Michael Webb is the Managing Director of whole of market mortgage brokerage Mortgage Republic. Having worked in the UK property industry since 2006 when he initially qualified as a mortgage broker, he has gained extensive experience throughout his career guiding property investor clients through the house buying and mortgage process. Over this time, he has helped hundreds of individuals build life changing property portfolios, many of which have been able to leave their employment to run full time property businesses or retire with a somewhat passive income from a rental portfolio.

A highly experienced mortgage broker himself, Michael leads a team of mortgage brokers based from their head office in Bury St Edmunds Suffolk. Helping property investors grow their portfolio and find financial independence has become a passion not only of Michael's but of his team as a whole. Mortgage Republic work with a spectrum of investors ranging from those just starting out, as a first time buyer, to those with multi million pound portfolios and hundreds of properties.

Michael has put together this guide for property investor buyers to better understand the process of buying an investment property and obtaining a mortgage. The tips, and information within this book should help any investment buyer navigate the buying process and quickly and simply obtain a mortgage offer from a lender*.

Find out more about Michael Webb and Mortgage Republic on their website:

www.mortgagerepublic.co.uk

It is important to point out that nothing in this book should be considered advice. The book is for information purposes only. If you require advice, we recommend seeking this out from a whole of market mortgage broker who can tailor advice to your specific needs.

Your property may be repossessed if you do not keep up with repayments on your mortgage.

*Subject to credit scoring and criteria.

1
Buy to let regulation

Buy to let mortgages in the UK are typically unregulated lending, classified as commercial lending. This is the case unless the tenant is a relative of the owner landlord and as such the mortgage would become a regulated buy to let. There are limited options for this type of lending [Please see the specific chapter].

However, in January 2017 the Prudential Regulation Authority [PRA] put in place underwriting standards to ensure that the buy to let market did not bring down the financial sector again like in the credit crunch of 2008

These standards included such things as increased focus on affordability through rental coverage increases, as well as further underwriting requirements for what are classed as portfolio landlords.

Under PRA guidance a Non-portfolio landlord will have 3 or less mortgaged buy to let properties, and a portfolio landlord will have 4 or more. This division and increased underwriting actually led to many lenders pulling out of the portfolio landlord market and only playing in the "amateur" market place.

A portfolio landlord can expect to have increased scrutiny placed upon their finances and their wider portfolio. Typical expectations are as follows:

A full portfolio schedule to be provided. This must include the following information:

- Property address
- Lender
- Loan amount
- Mortgage payment
- Rent received
- Purchase date
- A structured business plan must be provided.

Typically, this form will be provided by the lender, and specific information you must be able to provide will be around the strategy you are following. Such as are you investing for income or capital growth- or maybe both. What is your void management? How do you intend to deal with non-payers? Will you be managing the properties yourself or will you engage a letting agent to assist? What has your void history looked like?

On top of this you will be asked to provide a full assets and liabilities statement. This will include all debts, and assets you hold individually outside of the mortgage debts declared on the portfolio spreadsheet. This document will be used to assess your overall exposure when considering your income and outgoings to decide whether you as an individual would be a secure lending proposition.

Some of these documents can take some time to complete. Especially if you have a vast portfolio and therefore, it is highly advised that investors keep a version of each updated in their own format. Unfortunately, most mortgage lenders will require their own documents to be completed, and as such information will need to be copied on to the relevant forms but the good news is if it is to hand it will be a quicker job to perform.

As part of the PRA regulation of Buy to let mortgages there were increased affordability checks in the form of increased rental stress tests. The typical stress test a lender would expect the rent to cover the mortgage is:

5.5% X 145%

Working example:
£100,000 mortgage X 5.5% interest rate X 1.45% coverage = £7975 /12 = £664.58 rent required monthly
If the property cannot generate this level of rental there are a couple of options open to investors.

1. Top slicing. Some lenders will allow a top up of sorts from earned income to cover some or all of the shortfall. How much and availability of this feature is lender specific and is actually a real niche within the market place.
2. Like for like remortgages are often considered at much more relaxed stress rates
3. 5 year fixed rates. Some lenders reduce their requirement, down to the payrate interest at 1.25% in some really relaxed circumstances on 5 year deals. This is because their interpretation of the PRA guidelines is that the longer term

stability in the mortgage payments demonstrates affordability for a sufficient amount of time for them to relax the rental stress test. As property price increases have outstripped the rental increases, and as such reduced the yield on properties 5 year fixed have become a very popular choice for buy to let investors as this is sometimes the only way that sufficient funding can be raised for the purchase.

The rental calculations can also be affected by the applicants' tax status as either a lower rate tax payer or a higher rate tax payer. For lenders this has become exceptionally important because of the changes in the way that rental income is now taxed and how mortgage interest relief is dealt with. The reality of these changes is that a higher rate tax payer will end up with a significantly lower amount of net income post tax than a lower rate tax payer when we look at the rental income being received. Therefore, it is important for lenders to account for this when looking at ability to pay the mortgage payments.

Lenders will also be looking much more closely at your overall financial position. Have you increased unsecured debt over the last 6-12 months? Have you rapidly borrowed money to grow a portfolio.

Lenders appetites to loan money will of course differ with each lender's plans and goals for the year, along with their specific criteria however they will all need to demonstrate they are operating responsible lending.

Case study example:

An experience landlord with ownership of one buy to let was looking to buy a row of 5 separate terrace houses. The mortgages were placed all with the same lender as they initially agreed to lend on all 5 properties, and agreed it was acceptable to do so to this applicant. However, on full underwriting the application fell fowl of responsible lending criteria and as such only 3 of the 5 mortgages were offered, with the final 2 declined. The applicant subsequently raised the finance with another lender who agreed lending to them on 2 properties was acceptable, even though they had only just completed on 3 purchases.

The above demonstrates that sometimes risk needs to be spread across lenders to achieve the desired outcome, but also that doing too much too quickly can also make lenders nervous. The above applicant was going from amateur rules to professional portfolio rules with one transaction and this can sometimes be seen as a step too far too soon.

MICHAEL WEBB

2
Types of Buy to Let Mortgage

Regulated Buy to Let

Most buy to lets in the UK will fall under the banner of unregulated [by the FCA] transactions. Even though there is now PRA requirements on affordability for lenders to follow. Some however will be classed as regulated transactions and this is where a relative of the owner is residing in the property. Where this is the case lending will be limited. Not many buy to let lenders allow this due to the increased requirements on the underwriting. Regulated buy to lets need to be fully underwritten as if they were residential mortgages and therefore affordability checked in much more depth.

There is however lending within this market place currently available.

Consumer Buy to Let

An application will mostly be classed as a consumer buy to let if the landlord is being classed as an accidental landlord. An example will be if a property owner decides to rent out their own home and buy another [Let to Buy] or if an inherited property is rented out. Typically, the classification would be on initial ownership of the property the landlord did not initially intend to rent the property.

Most lenders will do some enhanced checks on this type of transaction and some may carry additional affordability checking. This will especially be true when a let to buy transaction is being completed.

Business Buy to Let

This is a typical buy to let transaction. The purchaser is buying the property as an investment to receive a rental income. The sole intention of the transaction is commercial from the outset and as such is underwritten on a non-regulated basis, subject to the PRA affordability guidelines.

3
Limited Company Buy to let

Since the changes in the way that rental income is being taxed limited company buy to let's have surged in popularity. This guide is not a taxation guide, so I will not go in to detail here on the changes, but below is an outline of the changes in how mortgage interest relief is being dealt with for individuals, and how a limited company may be beneficial. Of course, discussing this with a qualified tax advisor for your own specific situation is very important.

Changes are being phased in over a period of time. By the time we reach April 2020 you will no longer be able to claim tax relief on your rent received for interest paid. Instead you will receive a new tax credit which is less generous than the current scheme

and will significantly increase tax liability for higher rate tax payers.

The sliding scale which is in place is as follows:

In the 2017-18 tax year, you can claim 75% of your mortgage interest tax relief
In the 2018-19 tax year, you can claim 50% of your mortgage interest tax relief
In the 2019-20 tax year, you can claim 25% of your mortgage interest tax relief
In the 2020-21 tax year, you can claim 0% of your mortgage interest tax relief and the new system falls in to place in its' full force.

The remaining amount of your mortgage interest will qualify for the new qualifying tax credit as the years progress until you reach 2020/21 when 100% will be on the new system. This is a staged increase in taxation. As time goes on portfolio landlords who are higher rate tax payers with property in their own name will see their net of tax income decrease significantly overtime.

The above has been the leading factor for the increased popularity of limited company mortgages for buy to lets. Under current legislation this enables property owners to still offset 100% of their mortgage interest costs as a cost of the business, and then withdraw the profit as a dividend. The importance of tax advice in this area cannot be stressed enough. It's important to point out profits will be taxed as well as dividends. Therefore, a professional property accountant should discuss your plans with you to determine which strategy from a tax point of view would be best for you.

Limited company criteria

It is firstly important to point out that whilst a limited company is supposed to limit the liability of the shareholders and directors, borrowing a buy to let mortgage under these terms will require you to sign away those protections under the personal director guarantee you will be required to sign as part of the mortgage application and legal process.

Lenders who operate within this market, which whilst is growing, is still a niche in the buy to let sphere, require the individual directors and shareholders to be underwritten as if the application was in their own names. It will be the credit scores and profile of the individuals which is checked. It will be the earned income of the individuals which needs to meet the criteria set out by the lender and it will be the individuals who will be fully responsible for repaying the mortgage.

The limited company will need to have the correct SIC codes, and we therefore suggest advice is taken when forming the company. The company will need to be a special purpose vehicle [SPV] and not a trading company. There are some lender options for trading companies, but they are few and far between.

There is no trading time required. You can set the company up today, and as long as it can be searched on company's house and be seen as active you can apply for a limited company buy to let mortgage.

The sic codes required are one or all of the following:

68100 Buying and selling of own real estate

68209 Other letting and operating of own or leased real estate

68320 Management of real estate on a fee or contract basis

Typically, lenders will allow a maximum of 4 directors or shareholders on any company.

Company bank account

All direct debits for mortgage payments must be paid from a bank account in the company name. Unlike personal bank accounts which can easily be set up online and very quickly, a company bank account can take some time. In fact, I have known it to take 6+ weeks just to get an appointment to see the advisor to open the account. It is because of the increased due diligence required on company bank accounts that the delays occur with these. Advice is therefore you open a bank account with the bank you personally bank with. This should speed up due diligence as some has already been done on you as an individual. Mortgages will not be offered without the correct bank account being set up, and the direct debit mandate signed and the lender in possession of a direct debit in place.

Personal guarantee and legal advice

All limited company buy to let mortgages will require a director and shareholder personal guarantee. To double lock this down the lender will ensure you fully understand what you are signing by insisting you receive independent legal advice and confirm that this has occurred to them in writing

This will come at an additional cost to you and will need to typically be done by a separate solicitor to that who is doing the conveyancing as they are acting for the company.

Some lenders have a slightly more relaxed view on which solicitor is giving the independent advice and do not mind it being the same as that who is doing the conveyancing, which does make the process more streamlined and expedient.

Funding the deposit

When you purchase via a limited company you will need to fund the deposit via the limited company. Where the company is new and hasn't got retained profits to use the lenders will ask for the deposit to be funded from one of a few ways. There are some which are not acceptable, and I will cover these too.

Typically, a lender would expect the funds to be coming from the savings of the directors, and being director loaned to the limited company. In essence this sits in the same way as if you bought in your own name.

Some lenders will allow a gifted deposit from a direct family member. Direct would be parents, grandparents, and siblings. Of course, it might also be a spouse as the funds may be in a spouse's bank account and the spouse is not on the limited company ownership due to the tax advice you received.

Some lenders- but very few it must be added, will accept an intercompany loan. It is understood that this can have significant tax savings for individuals who own other limited companies which trade, and they derive income from. The reason being is that dividend tax does not need to be paid, and the money can move across from one company to another, meaning that the amount available is higher as no tax is due- although the loan is made after corporation tax is paid. It is important again to stress individual tax advice should be sort here.

A popular source of buy to let deposit has become pensions. This could be the 25% tax free lump sum or the whole pension fund, of which an element will be taxed.

Significant advice should be before doing anything with your pension fund, and this is only to explain that these funds are acceptable, and not to indicate it is appropriate for you to do so.

What source is not acceptable?

Angel finance: This is getting a random, non-related individual to loan the deposit to your company for a rate of interest return. This would constitute 100% lending in the eyes of the lender and as such is not acceptable. Please see the Angel Finance chapter for the best way to utilise this source of funds.

Unsecured finance: This would be in the form of an unsecured loan, or credit card drawdown facility. Many courses will teach you to take out multiple credit cards and draw down on 0% for an arrangement fee leave the money in your account for 3 months and then say it is savings and apply for a mortgage. Not only would this constitute mortgage fraud, potentially black listing you with buy to let lenders it is also just terrible advice.

However, there is nothing stopping you utilising these funds to buy for cash, and remortgaging to pay the debt off once the property has been refurbished and increased in value. Of course, you need to source a property which is cheap enough for you to purchase on you available credit card balances which can be drawn down.

It is important to state that the original source of the funds must be established, proven and documented to the lender for money laundering and terrorist financing regulations. I have seen too many people over the years trying to be clever with the source of deposit and trying to actually hide the original source and they always come unstuck with an application should they have found a broker willing to place the case whose compliance hasn't required them to ask the right questions.

4

The Angel Investor

With the rise of limited company usage and therefore a much more commercial and entrepreneurial outlook on property investing it has become very popular for property investors to seek out angel investors to fund their projects. This strategy poses some issues and has some pitfalls which all property investors should be aware of.

Whilst it is of course great marketing speak to say to people you wish to attend your training courses and seminars on property investing that you can use other people's money and none of you own to build a property portfolio, it is not quite as simple as these course's will lead you to believe. There are also some important aspects to be aware of.

As this is a financing guide, let us start with the angel investor being used as a contributor for the deposit. The main issue here is that the fund's origin needs to be established and declared to the buy to let lender.

Buy to let lenders will typically have no issue with a gifted deposit from a direct relative. But this must be a true gift. No lending- even received from a family member will typically not be acceptable as this would be classed as 100% lending.

Therefore, most angel investments are utilised for cash purchases. However, bridging companies may take a more relaxed approach to an investment being made into the company.

It is important to stress that if you are taking any form of angel investment it is yourself that is responsible to adhere to anti money laundering and terrorist financing regulations. You must establish the ID and proof of address of the individual. You must also establish the origin and source of the funds and must retain vigilant records on file that you have a process in place, and you have done your due diligence on the individuals and the funds. Failure to do this will leave you wide open to potential prosecution should there be any issues in the future.

I would always recommend a solicitor be engaged to help with this due diligence and to help draw up the angel investment contract.

5

Attracting Angel Investors

Professionalism is key when you are looking to attract potential investors to your company. Having an investment prospectus along with case studies of previous projects will of course add to this professionalism and instill trust and build rapport with your target audience. Crowd funding sites can also be great places to source investment from a range of individual investors looking to limit their risk on any single project.

Assessing your market place will also be important. Everyone seems to be offering 8-12% interest to invest in their projects. Some of these offers are for 12 months, some for longer. IE a fixed return of 12% over an 18 month period unless paid sooner.

Differentiating your proposition will be key to attracting cash investors who are looking for a return on their money hands free.

We frequently see investors spamming their facebook timeline with opportunities to invest with them. In our opinion it would be a risky investment to make off the back of a facebook post. A better strategy might be to hold an investors event. This would be a free event in a hotel, which might cost you a bit of money to set up and get going. Of course, if you are not willing to invest even a few hundred pounds on putting on some form of insight evening, then this might even come across to the people you are approaching as an attitude not conducive with achieving a desired outcome in an entrepreneurial world.

Within the 2 hour event for example you present your company, and your company's results. The results you have achieved for yourself and for your investors to date. If you are a new company and this is your first round, you will need to look very professional, but most of all honest and authentic. Don't try to be something you are not.

It would be a much better use of social media to present this free event, rather than just posting:

"£50,000 needed for 12 months, 8% return on offer, 1st charge on property offered - PM me"

6

HMO Mortgages

The HMO market has been through some changes recently. New regulations and planning requirements have come in to force and therefore for those looking to convert a property to an HMO the legislation and regulations are much more stringent.

As long as you are not a first time buyer there is a product in the market place for you to apply for. However, most HMO mortgages will require you to be an experienced landlord and the definition of experienced will change lender to lender. The range goes from 1 property for a year, to multiple properties owned and operated for over 3 years.

HMO mortgages are underwritten in the same way as a vanilla buy to let, with some added extras. Article 4 areas will require planning documents to be supplied and where the property is required to be licensed a license will need to be provided as part of the application.

The good news is that rent is worked out in the same formula as the single let property, and as such the calculations are much easier to achieve due to the higher rent achieved by multiples of room rates.

Converting to HMO

Since the licensing and article 4 changes have come in to force in 2018 HMO lenders require the property to be ready to go as an HMO when purchased. Therefore, the strategy for converting the property into a HMO will need to involve a purchase utilising either cash or a development bridging deal. The property can then be fully converted in to a compliant HMO property and then remortgaged at the 6 month ownership point on to a HMO deal.

HMO commercial valuations

It is often requested that HMOs have commercial valuations. This is because in theory these will come back higher than a bricks and mortar value and therefore investors will be able to take out more funds to recycle through their business.

There are a few types of valuations that could be carried out, and unfortunately as an applicant you cannot pick which one will be utilised. The surveyor will be the sole decision maker on which is most suitable for the property in question.

Bricks and Mortar – residential valuation

If you are multi letting a family home with little or no change to the property, then this valuation is mostly likely what will be used. The property is in essence a residential family dwelling, which needs little change for it to become that again.

Bricks and Mortar – Small HMO

A good example of this type of valuation will be where residential dwelling has been converted to an HMO but has had some works done such as all room converted to ensuite.

Maybe the property has been reconfigured to increase the rooms. What is most likely here is that the surveyor will value the property at bricks and mortar value plus an element considering the costs to convert back to a standard family home.

Bricks and Mortar – Large HMO

Larger HMOs where much more work has been done may well have an element of the rental received and the commercial value of the property considered to increase the value.

This is a hybrid really of the commercial value and the bricks and mortar and we see this most in HMOs of 6-7 bedrooms which could not very easily or economically be converted back to single dwellings.

Commercial valuation- Large HMO

Typically, you will be looking upwards of 8 rooms to get a full commercial valuation. However, bear in mind what I said in our middle option, which is that a larger HMO may also have an element of bricks and mortar and an element of commercial. Like a hybrid.

A full commercial valuation would be of a property that is very difficult to convert back to a single dwelling or has never been a single dwelling- an office block conversion for example. This type of property is likely to be valued on a relevant multiple of its annual rent. No lender has a set 10X rent [for example] structure, and it is an urban myth that certain lenders do. The business development managers of these lenders actually joke about it with brokers frequently. That does not mean that quite be coincidence the valuation will not come out very close to such a multiple of the annual rent.

7
Rental Calculations

The rental calculation used by a lender will depend on a few things. Firstly, the lender's interpretation of the PRA regulations, and also the type of transaction you are undertaking.

A base level rental calculation would be seen as: Mortgage amount X 5.5% X 145% = rental required.

As property prices have increased and rental levels have not kept pace this calculation has become harder and harder to actually hit.
Therefore, within the market place there are variations on this calculation to allow for a lower rent received to mortgage amount borrowed. Ways to achieve this are:

A like for like remortgage may have a much lower requirement. Like for like means no capital raising.

A 5 year fixed rate may also carry a lower calculation of:

Mortgage Amount X payrate [+x] X125% = rental required.

I have put in payrate + x because some lenders will utilise the payrate, whilst some may say it is the payrate plus a set amount – for example 1%.

Some lenders also still fully affordability check the application irrelevant of the rental coverage.

Top slicing

Top slicing is a term used by lenders to describe utilising income to top up the short fall on the rental calculation. Any deficit in rent received can be factored in to an affordability model and therefore earned income can be utilised to achieve the borrowing required. For top slicing to be used typically a higher than average income will need to be present, with lenders setting a minimum income received from earnings [employed/self-employed] for this option to be considered.

Portfolio coverage

Portfolio landlords- those with 4 or more mortgage buy to let properties, will also need their portfolio to meet the requirements set out by the lenders for rental coverage and overall loan to values.

Criteria in this section varies massively from lender to lender, and also portfolio size is key. Portfolios typically will need to be under 75% loan to value and fit the required criteria for rental coverage. However, some lenders in the market place do not concern themselves too much with the background portfolio as long as the rent is covering the payments and it is profitable.

8

How to Raise 100% Finance

It is really important for me to give some background on this structure and the criteria you will need to hit for this to even be considered by a lender. I must also add, there are not many lenders who are going to consider this, and the whole deal is dependent on valuation of the property stacking up.

Lenders will want to see that there is a commercial reason for the undervalue purchase. This is for a multitude of reasons- fraud, and money laundering being near the top of that list.

Typically, when I have done this type of transaction in the past it has been where a bulk discount is being applied because a buyer is buying multiple properties from the same vendor. This is therefore easy to prove an economic and commercial reason for the discounted purchase price.

Loan to values will be restricted as well typically to 70% or below, meaning for this to be a total no cash deposit deal the property will need to be 30% under confirmed market value. Of course, if the deal is only 10% under, that 10% can be utilised towards the total 30%, meaning only 20% cash needs to be input to the deal.

It is really important to say that you will not be able to just find a deal on rightmove, negotiate a discount and apply for a mortgage under this scheme. The lenders will just reject the application and request a cash deposit.

The criteria for these types of deals are not written or published but are deep within a lenders' criteria, and therefore not known to many. Lenders do not want an influx of these types of applications.

It is highly unlikely you will be considered for this type of financing structure unless you are a professional portfolio landlord with a demonstrable track record, and a history of success in property. It is not a solution for a first time landlord with no funds.

9
Air BNB & Holiday Lets

Serviced accommodation and holiday lets have become a very popular way to invest in to property. By no means are they a hands-off investment, in fact the complete opposite with a much higher level of management and involvement needed. Serviced accommodation for example could mean checking in 7 different people a week to your property if the property is rented on a nightly basis.

There are some significant things to consider when undertaking this type of investment. Most importantly are any covenants on the property in question. Leasehold apartments in particular in city centres, which would obviously be attractive to potential Air BNB renters, may come with covenants within the lease that prevent you from operating the property in this fashion.

It is critical you have this checked by your legal representation.

From a financing standpoint, lenders will still have a rental calculation you will be required to meet.

Typically, this will be the mortgage X 5.5% X 145% = rent required. However, what will be significantly different is how that rent is worked out. Criteria differs lender to lender, so I feel it is best to run through a few of the scenarios.

Firstly, and quite common you will be given permission to holiday let the property on a holiday let mortgage but the rental as a family let, on a monthly basis must cover the calculation set by the lender.

Alternatively, lenders may ask for the weekly holiday rental for low, mid and high season. They ill then average this to get an annual average and then multiple by a set number of weeks – say 30, to allow for some vacant weeks, and then divide this by 12 to give a monthly income for the property.

Most holiday let mortgages also allow an element of usage by the owner. Typically, up to 4 weeks a year. Allowing the owner of the property to own their own holiday home in a location they chose and enjoy, whilst renting it for the other weeks of the year to gain an income.

Furnished holiday let income is treated differently to ordinary buy to let income for tax purposes and is treated as a trading income under current legislation. Therefore, the mortgage interest relief is better than that of a standard buy to let owned in your own name. Obviously, this is not a taxation guide and I hold no tax qualifications, so you should check your own tax situation with a qualified professional along with the current legislation which is fluid and changing frequently.

Due to the need to attract potentially 365 individual clients to rent the property, or at best 48 – assuming you use the property for 4 weeks yourself, it is important to understand the local holiday let market and the demand for the types of property you intend to acquire. It is really important to have a marketing plan in place and probably holiday agents on board with access to the marketplace. A lot more work and research will need to be conducted on these types of deals prior to jumping in to a transaction.

MICHAEL WEBB

10

Different Types of Mortgage Brokers/Advisor

As if the UK mortgage market was not complex enough for people the types of advisors you can use are varied as well. There are plenty of options and routes for applying for a mortgage in the UK. Here I will run through the most common for you to help you better understand the types of organisation you will come across in your search for a mortgage advisor.

It's important to say that this should be one of the first things an advisor runs through with you under their scope of service, and terms of business. It's unlikely they won't but if you are in that situation you need to ask.

Bank Based- Single tied advice

Typically approaching a bank or building society direct will result in you receiving advice about a single product line from that provider. They are tied to that bank [Barclays for example] and will not compare how that product sits within the overall marketplace for you. They have no obligation to.

Most banks and building societies will have a range of products, but will have their own set criteria, and affordability calculations and as such you will find there is a significant difference in how much one offers to another. Of course, you can visit every branch in town [If your town still has a branch] or go on every bank's website, and do some serious leg work yourself to see what they might lend, or what their products are. Checking whether you match their criteria will probably involve at least a conversation with one of the representatives.

It is important to note there are several lenders within the marketplace who only deal with mortgage brokers and you cannot go direct to them. This is more common in the niche markets of adverse credit and buy to let, but lenders such as Accord Mortgages, Platform, The Mortgage Works [Part of Nationwide BS] are intermediary only and as such you can only gain access to their products via a broker authorised to transact with them.

There are many more than those 3 mentioned. Access via a mortgage broker only is particularly common in the buy to let and investment market. Much more so than the private residential mortgage market.

Brokers- Panel of lenders

Many brokers operate from panels of multiple lenders. These panels will fluctuate in size, and will have been created for different reasons ranging from product availability and criteria, right down to the commissions the brokers can negotiate for restricting the distribution. Most panel broker work with between 20 & 50 lenders.

The benefits against going to a bank directly are clear. You will get an overview of a multitude of lenders which will mean you have done some shopping around to ensure you are not paying more than you need to. These brokers will be working with the same lenders frequently and as such will be familiar with their lending criteria. They are however not checking everyone.

As a property investor you may find that if the broker is working from a very limited panel without the ability to go off of that panel to place business your options for lending with such brokers can run out quickly as you meet maximum lending with particular lenders. Levels a lender is willing to commit to an individual investor will vary, and the speed at which that investor wishes to progress to that point will also be a factor in deciding whether lending is available.

Brokers- Whole of market

Some brokers are not tied to any lender or panel. They can go to any lender in the UK that will work with an intermediary. It is fair to say that the majority will, but there are still some brands within the industry which do not. Typically, however they have a brand within the larger organisation which does. Two prime examples of this would be Lloyds Bank who do not, but Halifax who are part of the Lloyds banking group who do work with intermediary partners. The same applies to First Direct who do not and HSBC [their parent company] who do. It is fair to say most buy to let lender work with intermediaries, and some exclusively so, meaning you cannot approach them directly.

The benefits of a whole of market broker are that you are truly checking every option which would be open to you. This may be especially important if your case is slightly tricky for any reason, you have adverse credit history, or you just want to be 100% sure you are not paying more than you need to be.

Even though whole of market brokers can go to any lender who will work with them it is also important to note that some lenders are only just entering the market and as such restrict the distribution.

Therefore, they pick and choose the broker firms they make their products available to. These may be whole of market or panel broker firms. Excellent current examples of this would be HSBC, Tesco bank, M&S bank, and Sainsburys bank.

Appointed Representatives & Directly Authorised

Many broker firms, even large ones, are appointed representatives of much larger organisations. This can bring benefits to both the client and the broker firm.

The broker firm will benefit from a larger support structure and compliance structure. Although will have to operate within the guidelines set by the principal firm. However, in exchange for this they will potentially have access to exclusive deals negotiated as part of a wide economy of scale otherwise not available to them. They may also have access to exclusive lenders due to the lenders having more confidence in the compliance structure of the principal firm.

Some firms however will be directly authorised. If this firm is a very large firm, potentially it will also have appointed representatives. However, if it is a smaller firm there is the possibility whilst it may be able to market itself as whole of market, there will be lenders in the market place who will feel it is not economically viable to do the required due diligence on the firm due to the low levels of business they may receive, and as such that broker will not be able to place business with some lenders.

Benefits of course to the broker is that they can set their own compliance guidelines, within the FCA rulebook. They will however be directly answerable to the FCA.

There is no right way to operate. It will be down to the individual company to decide, and both ways are very viable and successful. However, as an investor do your own due diligence on the firm you are looking to work with and check just how "whole of market" they really are.

Broker Permissions

Although a broker may be whole of market, they may only hold certain advising permissions. For example, they may only lend on first charge residential and buy to let mortgages. This is a very common option for mortgage brokers.

Some brokers may only be set up to deal with bridging finance or second charge lending. Whilst of course you will likely have commercial finance specialists as well.

Some firms will hold permissions for all of these streams of lending but will likely have departments that deal with the specialisms so to have experts in that field dealing with clients. Bridging finance is very different to term buy to let finance.

Due to the permissions a firm may hold to provide a full scope to their clients they may also set up partnerships with other firms where there are reciprocal agreements that they work together where needed and one firm takes control of the advice that the client requires. This is also a very popular set up. Large Appointed representative networks will provide outlets to their AR firms through large companies which have had significant due diligence conducted on them to ensure good customer outcomes.

Broker fees

It is very typical nowadays for brokers to charge a fee for their service as well as receive a commission [typically called a procuration fee] from the lender upon completion. These fee structures can vary dramatically broker to broker and should definitely be something you factor in to your decision making when deciding on who to use.

Broker fees can come in the following forms

Fixed fee: Example £495. Paid at time of advice, application, offer or completion, or a combination of 2 or more.

Percentage fee: Example 1.5% of the loan. Paid at time of advice, application, offer or completion, or a combination of 2 or more.

Some brokers will charge "lifetime advice fees" meaning you only pay a fee to them once and can use their services as many times as you wish. However, beware of additional admin fees which are not classed as advice fees which may apply in these situations.

Typically going to a bank direct will not incur any broker fees as no product comparison or broking has occurred.

It is important to point out that most mortgages nowadays are transacted via a broker. Typically, 80% plus- including buy to let and residential lending. This is even higher when just looking at buy to let applications in isolation, and many buy to let lenders can only be accessed via an intermediary and not directly. This is because the lenders prefer to market via a channel which will sift out applicants who would not meet the lenders criteria. The broker's job is to place the applicant with the most relevant and affordable lender.

As an investor broker fees will fall under the same category for tax as your mortgage interest, and as such are not as tax efficient anymore. They could be a very large expenditure for you if you are transacting a lot of mortgages annually. Working with the same broker and building a longerterm relationship, whether they charge a lifetime fee or not is always a good recommendation. This familiarity with your situation will speed up your applications, and the rapport you build will give you the opportunity to potentially negotiate a lower fee per application, or possibly a no fee application.

It is likely that broker fees for buy to let mortgages will be lower than those for bridging finance or development finance. The latter are really unregulated commercial lending and fees are likely to be around the 2% level of gross borrowing. However, it is true to say these vary vastly across the industry.

There can be an attitude in the market that brokers are paid by the lenders so they should not receive a fee from the clients as well. It is our experience that if the lender procuration fee was not paid the overall fee charged to the clients would be much higher, and as such the lender is only acting to keep the client costs down, rather than replace them.

The fee in essence is actually for doing the work for the lender and not the work for the client. For example, taking compliance responsibility for the advice being given, which does come with an element of risk to the broker.

MICHAEL WEBB

11
Surveys and Mortgage Valuation

As part of any mortgage application the mortgage lender will require a RICS [Royal Institute of Chartered Surveyors] surveyor to value the property. There are typically 3 levels of survey and valuation which you can chose from. The mortgage lender will only receive the valuation report in any instance. It is possible from the report that the lender receives that further investigations may be required. I will also cover what types of reports are commonly requested by lenders, and the potential implications for your purchase they may have.

Basic Mortgage Valuation

This is a basic report, typically 2-3 pages long and covers very basic aspects of the property condition. The surveyor is assessing the properties suitability for lending only. Different lenders will request different things be checked. The report will provide an official valuation for the property – however will not state if the surveyor feels you are paying less than it is worth unless this is a significant difference [Which raises money laundering concerns]. They will of course state whether they feel you have agreed to pay too much for the property. This will of course mean you will either need to increase your deposit or reduce the purchase price agreed with the vendor. The latter is not always possible, and neither is raising the deposit. Frequently sales fall through due to this.

The report is instructed by the lender, is basically for the lenders own information and will provide little information relevant to the buyer. However, unless the mortgage product comes with a free valuation it is paid for by the applicant, and the cost will vary depending on the price [which assumes size] of the property.

If you are applying for a buy to let mortgage your report will also state whether the property is lettable, the market rent that could be achieved, and the marketability and demand in the rental market local to the property for this unit.

In addition to this if the property is an HMO, or intended to be, it is likely that caveats will be entered that the property valuation is on the assumption that correct planning and licenses are held.

Homebuyers Survey

This is a 20 to 25 page report which will go in to much more depth than a basic mortgage valuation. The report will use a traffic light system of Red, Amber and Green. Red meaning the item needs immediate attention, amber meaning that remedial work be required in the near future and green meaning satisfactory condition and no issues.

Having spoken to many surveyors over many years they would recommend these reports for properties over 10 years old because those that are younger are still covered by a new build warranty such as NHBC.

If a homebuyers report is instructed it is common for it to be done as an upgrade to the basic mortgage valuation, and have the same surveyor conduct the report. This is a financially beneficial way of operating and will typically keep your costs down. The lender would only receive the basic mortgage valuation and not the homebuyers report which would be sent directly to you the buyer.

A homebuyers report is commonly instructed on purchases and is some what referred to as "a survey" by the general public. It is a useful report for establishing the condition of the property, and at times has been very useful in renegotiating the price when issues are found to be present.

Full Structural survey

This is a full structural report on the property. Typically, this will be requested if you have specific concerns about the structure or the property is of a certain age- say 100 years old. Older and significantly larger properties often have these types of survey, which involve the surveyor spending significant time at the property investigating any potential issues.

It's important when buying a home that you discuss the types of survey with your mortgage broker and choose wisely which one would be most suitable.

Other reports

It is important to note that chartered surveyors are not a jack of all trades. What is checked in the property is limited. They are not doing an electrical check, or gas safety check. They will not check your heating works, or that there is no issues with the water and drainage.

Off the back of any of the survey report or basic mortgage valuation the surveyor may suggest further reports be obtained prior to the lender considering the property as adequate security for the mortgage.

Added to the list of reports below it can also be very beneficial to have your appointed builder do a walk round and schedule of works for you on the property. Their expertise may be beneficial in assessing any possible pitfalls in refurbishments you are considering. Their working technical knowledge may actually be considered more beneficial than an upgraded survey, however that is something you should consider on a property by property basis and is not a recommendation not to have a more detailed survey undertaken.

Typically, these reports will fall in to the following categories:

Structural Engineers report

Where the property may have signs of structural issues or movement such as subsidence the surveyor may request a structural engineers report before confirming their value. This report will check the structural adequacy of the property, check whether any movement is current or historic, and generally check the building isn't going to fall down any time soon.

The reports can be requested on the whole property or just sections of the property. The structural engineer will produce a report, at your cost, which the lender will then have assessed by their surveyor.

They will determine from this whether the property is adequate security for lending.

Different lenders and products such as term buy to let and bridging, will have different criteria on the required structural integrity of the building. It is common for buyers who come across serious issues who decide they wish to proceed still, to change from a buy to let product to a heavy refurbishment bridging product, and remortgage at a later stage once the work has been adequately completed.

Damp and Timber report

Sometimes the survey will bring up evidence of damp, wood worm, or fungal issues in the timbers. If this is the case the surveyor will request a damp and timber report from a specialist in this field before making a decision on whether the property is appropriate security for lending.

It is very common for these reports to be requested, and also very common for them to come back with no issues found or only very minor issues. Surveyors seem to deem this a risk area and are exceptionally cautious and as such request them a lot. Particularly if a property is in need of work, is old or is showing any signs at all of damp.

Electrical survey

The surveyor as already mentioned is not an electrician. Due to this it is typical for a homebuyers report to suggest you obtain an electrical report from a suitably qualified individual. If there are any specific concerns around the electrics within the property, then this report may be requested to establish the suitability of the property to be mortgaged.

Gas safety certificate

When you rent a property, it needs to come with a gas safety certificate to ensure you are not being put in danger from the gas appliances within the property. Strangely when you buy a property this is not required. Most people would ask their solicitor to obtain the latest servicing report for the boiler and heating system however.

Therefore, it may be prudent to have a gas report done on the property, or at minimum have the gas boiler serviced and heating checked as soon as you acquire and move in to your new home.

Asbestos report

Some older properties may still have elements of the property which would be suspected of having asbestos within them. It is likely in this case that the surveyor will request an asbestos report, including an outline of costs to remove and update that element of the property safely. It will also confirm whether the surveyors suspicions were correct or not. They tend to air on the side of caution here, and quite frequently in my experience no asbestos is found.

All of these additional reports will come at additional cost, which will need to be covered by yourself. Most estate agents are very well versed in dealing with these reports and will have a list of tried and tested local suppliers who they can put you in touch with should the need arise.

MICHAEL WEBB

12

Ways to repay your mortgage

Historically there has been 2 ways you can repay your mortgage. Either on a capital repayment basis, or on an interest only basis. In this section I will run through how each of these work; including the benefits of each, and add in some real 2018 criteria that will help you narrow down your choice.

Capital repayment

A capital repayment mortgage is where each month you pay a little bit of capital and a little bit of interest [Or a big bit of interest to start with] to pay your mortgage down to zero owed at the end of the full term – say over 25 years for this example.

Interest is typically charged on mortgages on a daily basis, based on an annual rate dependent on the type of product you are on. [See the products section for more details] At the beginning of your mortgage your payment will be made up of more interest and less capital, because the balance you owe is higher, and therefore there is more interest due that month. As you start to pay the mortgage down, the interest due reduces and as such more each month is paid off the debt until finally you owe zero at the end of the 25 years. [Of course, longer and shorter terms are available]

Interest Only

As the name suggests each month you only service the interest on the mortgage and the debt does not reduce. This does give you therefore lower monthly payments. However, it is important to stress you need to be able to pay the debt off at the end of the 25 years. Many people have come in to difficulties with this, and as such very large deposits are required as well as high levels of equity in monetary terms [For example 25% equity of a minimum of £150,000 is a common piece of criteria].

.

Overall you will also pay more interest this way, as you are always paying interest on the full amount borrowed, and not on a reducing balance.

To pay the mortgage off you would need to have an investment in place which would run alongside the mortgage and mature at the same time enabling you to use the funds to settle the debt. These would typically be something like an ISA, or endowment. History shows us that these types of investments when used to repay a mortgage have not achieved at the level they were expecting to [And were sold as back in the 1980s and 1990s] and therefore this is a high risk strategy for repaying your mortgage. Some people chose to use the sale of the property as the repayment vehicle for the mortgage and of course fluctuating house prices can leave you in a difficult situation if the property has not maintained its value or appreciated as expected during the mortgage term.

Interest only in the past was a common way for first time buyers to get on to the property market in an affordable way. However, nowadays it is very unlikely a first time buyer would take out an interest only mortgage due to the changes in criteria. Most first time buyers will nowadays take out a repayment mortgage.

If you have a lower deposit of under 25% then this will be the only option open to you anyway under current criteria.

Overpayments

Where it is affordable to do so we always recommend clients overpay their mortgage. Any payments reduce the capital owed immediately, and therefore help to pay the mortgage back quicker, reducing the amount of interest paid overall. Most mortgages have a 10% overpayment facility [of your current balance for the year] and some can be set up with unlimited overpayment facilities. Overpaying is an effective way to pay your mortgage off quicker than planned and pay less interest overall. Typically, this can be done on either an interest only or repayment mortgage. Overpayments can be made as a regularly increase to your monthly direct debit, or as one off lump sums.

13

Documents Required

For every application you will need to provide standard money laundering and anti-terrorism regulation documents. These consist of:

Proof of ID:
- Passport or driving license
- It is likely an electronic check will also be conducted on you

Proof of address:

- Dated within the last 3 months
- Utility bill, Council tax bill
- Bank statement which has been posted to you

Typically, mobile phone bills are not acceptable

A broker may also conduct an electronic money laundering ID check on you, which will only pass if you are on the electoral roll.

Please note some lenders may require you to proof your residency at any address you have lived at for the last 3 years. Especially if you have not been registered on the electoral roll. Keep your bills if you are moving house.

Proof of Income- Employed

Have to had 6 months' pay slips and your P60.
It is likely you will only need 3 months, but if you have additional income on the payslip above a basic salary the lender may ask for a longer track record of it.

If you pay has changed recently- payrise etc, a letter from your employer outlining this
If you have been with your employer for a short period of time- say 6 months or less-Your employment contract is required

Proof of income – Self employed

If you are self-employed typically you will need to have a 2 year trading history. There are some lenders who accept 1 year.

To demonstrate your income you will need to obtain your SA302s for up to 3 years if possible and trading that long. To accompany them you will need your tax summary overviews. Your accountant can provide both these documents to you, alternatively if you do your own return then HMRC will post your SA302s to you- typically take 3 weeks to arrive, and you can download the tax summary overview from your online portal.

Proof of Income- Limited company directors over 20% shareholding

If you own more than 20%/25% of the company that employs you the lender will treat you as self-employed. They will therefore ask for your SA302s, and tax summary overviews. However, in addition they might also ask for the company accounts for the last 3 years also. This is to ensure the company can sustain paying you the salary and dividends you are currently taking on an ongoing basis.

Bank statements:

Online bank statements are perfectly acceptable. You should have a minimum of 3 months available and be ready to be asked for up to 6 months on occasions.

Online bank statements should show your name, address, and account number and sort code. In addition to this many may have a URL along the bottom indicating authenticity as a document produced from that particular banks' website.

Proof of deposit:

- Gifted deposit letter- if applicable
- Bank statements showing the build up of savings- up to a couple of years has been asked for in the case of very large deposits. Typically, 3-6 months is adequate.

Lenders are becoming much more vigilant on establishing the origin of funds, and the true source of an applicant's wealth. New regulations placed upon them are becoming quite taxing on the applicant who does not have clear records. We have seen some declines where lenders are not happy with evidence provided for deposit funds.

14
Type of mortgage Products

When you take out a mortgage there are a variety of products that you can chose from. These can sometimes be confusing, but over the coming pages I hope to outline each, along with the benefits and potential pitfalls of each. Establishing which is best for your situation can not be done by reading this book and a conversation with a qualified whole of market broker should be undertaken to guide you on which product best suits your needs.

Fixed rate

A fixed interest rate will give you a stable mortgage payment for a set duration in time. These timeframes are typically set at 2 year, 3 year, and 5 year intervals. However, whilst these are the most popular terms, there are longer term fixed rates of 7 and 10 years in the market place, and I have known lenders to offer 25 year fixed within my broking career. [Nationwide Building Society- some years ago]. A lot changes in 25 years, and as such these were not overly popular.

A fixed rate will offer stability in payments for a set period of time which makes budgeting easier. Especially if this is your first mortgage.

However, you will likely be tied in with an early repayment charge [A penalty of interest if you were to pay the mortgage off in full during the fixed rate period]. The stability provided may also come at a cost compared to other deals which might have interest rates that start lower, although cannot be guaranteed to stay that way.

Fixed rate mortgages have become very popular in the current low interest rate economy- although there is an argument that the historic stability of the bank of England base rate has actually cost people money by going on a fixed rate. This is not to say moving forward the same will apply.

They are very popular with investor buyers however due to the fact that investors know they will receive a fixed return over and above the mortgage payment in the form of rent received for a set period of time. This makes business planning and budgeting much easier.

Base Rate Tracker

A base rate tracking interest rate is one that is tied to the Bank of England's base rate. The interest tracks the base rate at a set amount above or below the bank of England's base rate depending on the product. For example, Base rate plus 2%

A base rate tracker may be a cheaper product initially to a fixed rate. It also may not. The downside of the product is that the rate you pay is reviewed monthly in line with the bank of England base rate reviews. If the rate is increased, the following month your mortgage payment will increase in line with any rate changes. Of course, if the base rate is reduced then your mortgage payment will reduce inline accordingly.

Therefore, there is a lack of stability in your payments if the bank of England base rate changes regularly, and you must be comfortable with fluctuating payments potentially.

The tracker rate can be set for a period of time- 2 years, 3 years etc, including up to a lifetime of the mortgage tracker.

You will likely be tied in with an early repayment charge [A penalty of interest] if you were to pay the mortgage off in full during the tracker rate period.

Lifetime trackers typically have an early repayment charge for the first few years up to 5 years, or no early repayment charge at all. They are popular therefore with people who wish to make large overpayments outside the usual 10%-20% allowances which can be found in the market place.

Standard Variable Rate

The standard variable rate is set by the lender and is unique to them [Although many are the same rate] Typically, the rate is higher than the fixed/tracker/discount product rate. The rate is determined by the internal economics of the bank or building society and is not tied to any external rate. However, most do increase it or reduce it by an amount [Not always equal to] the movement of the bank of England base rate. For example, a reduction in the bank of England rate of 0.25% may see a lender reduce their standard variable rate by 0.15% or 0.35%. They are not however obliged to do so- unless their mortgage contract states they will.

It is typical for there to be no early repayment charges on a standard variable rate.

This is a rate you will typically revert to when your deal ends. Very rarely is it available as a new mortgage product.

Discounted rate

A discounted rate is also a variable rate. It is a rate set as a discount against the standard variable rate for a set period of time – much like a tracker rate for 2 years, 3 years or 5 years. [Sometimes longer].
The product does provide a true discount against the standard variable rate. However, it is also a variable rate so there is a lack of stability, and as already discussed you are at the mercy of the lenders internal economics- not the bank of England base rate.

Caps and Collars

Some interest rates which are variable will have additional features such as being capped or collared. What this means in real terms is that a maximum rate the product can ascend to – a cap, is put on the product, providing an element of risk protection for borrowers. The rate for example may have a cap of 6% meaning it can go up and down but never above 6% during the capped rate period.

The same can apply at the other end. A collar can be placed on the product meaning that it will never descend below a set rate. For example, this could be 2%. Meaning no matter how low the rate could go your lowest interest rate will be 2%.

It is possible for both to apply, giving you the interest rate spread your mortgage will be within. This gives you an opportunity to benefit from rate reductions to some level and be protected from interest rate increases to a certain level as well.

Offset Mortgage

Offset mortgages are mortgage that have an account attached to them which may be a savings account or a current account. The product for this mortgage is often a variable rate, however there is the possibility it could be a fixed rate.

The balance of the attached account is offset against the debt of the mortgage, and no interest is paid on that element of the mortgage, and no interest is received on the balance in the attached account.

For example:
- £100,000 Mortgage
- £10,000 Savings
- £90,000 balance incurs interest charge

Of course, this is a good way to pay less interest on your mortgage and make your savings potentially work harder for you. However, things to consider are.
1. The interest rates involved. Are you paying a higher rate on the balance than you need to?
2. Compound interest on your savings. This is not occurring with these types of accounts.

These types of products come and go in the market and their popularity is currently not very high. However, they still hold a position in the UK market and could be the right choice for the right people.

For investors these types of products do offer a draw down like facility, however. Funds can be held within a savings account meaning that no interest is payable on the savings balance. This is immediately available to be utilised as deposits for purchases moving forward.

Many investors use an offset mortgage for this very purpose.
It is important to note offset mortgages are typically only available on residential mortgages, not buy to let.

Product fees

Some of the products mentioned above may come with a fee. This may be a set amount or a percentage of the loan amount. The product fee can either be paid up front or added to the loan in most cases. Of course, if you are adding a fee to the loan you will of course be paying interest on this fee over the course of your mortgage.

Banks and Building societies will typically offer a fee structure that varies with the interest rate and a range of products.

To illustrate this example their product range may look something like this:

- 2.19% £995 fee
- 2.39% £495 fee
- 2.59% No fee

What is important to establish is what is the best product rate and fee combination for yourself. A good broker will guide you through this process typically assessing the total cost of the deal over the initial benefit period. [2 years for a 2 year fixed for example].

This will very much be determined by the size of the loan. Paying a higher fee for a smaller loan to benefit from a 0.4% reduction in rate as per our example above may not recoup the £995 fee over the 2 year period. However, for a much larger loan if may well save a lot more than £995.

Therefore, it is important to engage in a conversation with your broker on what deal is the cheapest overall for you, and not just chase headline rates.

Important note:

Headline rates are really low rates that lenders put out in the market to gain media attention especially in rate comparison tables that are published in financial press and on comparison websites. However, these deals sometimes come with really high fees to offset the low interest rate and might not actually be the best deal in the marketplace for a particular borrower.

The above example was utilised for ease of explaining how the rate structures may work. It is important to stress that buy to let fees may be significantly higher than this and are very commonly a percentage of the borrowing amount ranging from 1% to 3% of the loan.

15

First time buyer – Buying to let

This is somewhat a niche market within the mortgage world. Typically, a mortgage lender would require you to be an owner occupier, or at least an owner of another buy to let property before considering you for this type of mortgage. However, it is an urban myth that you cannot buy a property to let out as a first time buyer. There are currently products available, and in this section, we will run through the typical criteria for an applicant to apply for this type of mortgage.

A buy to let property might be something to consider as a first time buyer especially if you live in an area where you are finding it unaffordable to get on to the property ladder. Typically, this will be affluent areas such as the South East. It has therefore become popular for first time buyers to purchase a property in a more affordable area such as Wales or the North East and let the property out.

This allows the buyer to achieve some home ownership and benefit from a potential income and capital appreciation that may occur. If all of the above occurs buyers could then sell the property for a larger cash deposit or continue receiving a rental income which could be used to pay the mortgage down.

Of course, tax will be due at the current rate for rent received. [Seek individual tax advice for this]

Most buy to let mortgages will have a minimum age to apply. This is typically 21 years old, or some have 25. They will also typically have a minimum income requirement, which is set at £25,000 for most lenders. It may be possible to source a first time buyer buy to let mortgage if you income is below this threshold but your options will be significantly limited.

A buy to let mortgage for a first time buyer will also require a much larger deposit in percentage terms than you will need for a residential mortgage. A residential mortgage typically would require a minimum of 5% deposit. Typically, a buy to let mortgage for a first time buyer will be set at 25%, hence most buyers would be looking at a property in a more affordable area, with a strong rental demand.

What is clear from the marketplace is there are limited options for this type of lending, and this is due to the risk involved. Buy to let mortgages are not regulated like residential owner occupier mortgages and as such go through less checks. However, for a first time buyer the lenders who offer these products are keen to close any affordability loop holes which may present themselves, and as such you need to fit their current residential affordability calculations for the loan you are requesting, as well as the buy to let criteria such as minimum incomes, rental calculations for coverage of mortgage payments, and minimum ages. Other things considered may be debt to income ratios.

Rental coverage

The rent received from any buy to let property will need to cover the mortgage payment at a set interest risk rate, by a certain percentage. Typically the calculation will look similar to this:

Mortgage @ 5.5% x 1.45/12 = Minimum Monthly Rent Required

A working example would look like this:

- £100,000 @5.5% = £5500
- X 1.45/12
- = £665 minimum require monthly rent

First time buyers taking out buy to let mortgage must be aware of the overall expenditure including the costs of where they currently reside. This is especially important if the buyer is currently in a rented property themselves. Mortgage payments and council tax need paying if the property is occupied or vacant. Council tax will be due by the owner if it is unoccupied. This type of property investment is a fairly simple one for buyers to get involved with, but that should not take away anything from the consideration about taking on further debts. You must also consider the impact the buy to let may have on any future intentions to get a residential home.

It must also be pointed out here as it is in our stamp duty section that the first time buyer exemption only applies if you intend to live in the property and as such getting a buy to let mortgage and renting the property would mean you would not receive this exemption. You would also need to consider when you bought your subsequent property- even if this was a residential home you are likely to have to pay the 3% surcharge for second properties.

Overall this is something worth considering if you are wanting to own a property, have an income and a deposit, but are unable to achieve the prices local to you. However, it is something we strongly advise you take professional guidance on before jumping in.

A Buy to Let Alternative

As a first time buyer wanting to dip their toe in to property investing and renting a good way to do this might be to buy a property as your main residency and live there whilst renting out the rooms. This strategy would work well for single individuals or couples without children. If you are able to buy something that is bigger than you require, such as a 3 bed property, you could rent the additional un-utilised bedrooms out to lodgers. This is perfectly acceptable under the terms and conditions of most residential mortgages.

This strategy is good for a few reasons.

1. You can potentially get a property with only a 5% deposit. There are even some 100% lending possibilities for first time buyers, or even shared ownership; the latter which is not available for buy to let.
2. The income you receive is very tax efficient under the current tax criteria. When renting rooms within your own home, the first £7500 in income received is tax free. Meaning you can rent 2 rooms at £70 each a week, and pay not income tax on that amount of money.
3. The additional income you receive can be used to save for further buy to let deposits, or pay the mortgage down quicker with overpayments, meaning less overall interest is paid, and potentially lower interest rates can be achieved quicker as you increase the property's equity and reduce your loan to value.

16
Types of Mortgage insurance

When taking out any debt is important to ensure no matter what happens in life you are able to pay that back, and more importantly keep your home. This is why you will always see the standard "Your home may be repossessed if you do not keep up repayments on your mortgage" warning everywhere someone is talking about mortgages. Banks will eventually take the keys back if you do not pay. As a landlord there is not only the responsibility to pay your debts, but to also ensure that whoever is tenanted in your property is not made homeless through your inability to pay mortgage debts. However, it can be the last thing that a new landlord considers when taking out a buy to let mortgage.

Our suggestion would be that you take advice at an early stage of your property investment journey to protect not only your assets, but your tenant's homes. Taking this professional approach to your financial management is important when investing in property.

There are plenty of life events that can cause homeowners and property investors issues with paying their mortgage. These events will result in a reduction or complete loss of your income, meaning that you are left to survive on reserve funds- which typically most people do not have an abundance of, and therefore issues occur with making committed payments.

These events could be things such as a death of a partner, completely removing their income, and causing issues with the surviving partner being able to maintain the expenditure which was committed to with 2 incomes, or possibly needing to reduce their own income and working hours due to an increase in child care requirement.

Another very important issue to look at is what protection your employer would provide if you were of sick. It is rare outside the public sector for companies to provide any long term sick pay, with most being approx. 1 to 3 months maximum.

Of course, there will be exceptions to this, however it is our experience that buyers understanding of what their employers will provide, and what government help they would receive is well off the mark when we start to investigate it. I can count numerous times I have been told someone has 6 months or 12 months sick pay, only to get their employment contract and find out it says 4 weeks, with an increase to 12 weeks at the absolute discretion of the employer, dependent on history of sickness, and term of service. There are some massive differences here in the protection your employer would provide.

Of course, redundancy is also an issue that people can face. This is something you can also look to negate risk for. However, taking out a policy to protect a buy to let mortgage is not possible.

The only thing you cannot protect against is being sacked from your job from things like gross misconduct. Mainly because this is a controllable aspect from yourself, and very much too high risk for insurance companies because you could just get yourself sacked to get a payout.

So, what can you do to protection yourself against these incidents that occur in our lives, and more frequently, and at younger ages than most believe to be the case.

Life Insurance

The most common protection people will take out is a decreasing term assurance [Life insurance] for a repayment mortgage or level term assurance to cover their interest only mortgage and ensure it is paid off if they were to die. This is probably the cheapest form of insurance. However, it is important to look outside of the mortgage as well when considering this type of cover. If a partner was to die, having the mortgage paid off will of course be a priority; especially if both incomes were needed for the mortgage and other outgoings to be affordable.

However, the family unit has now lost not only an income, but a member which could mean the surviving partner needs to reduce their own working time, and subsequent income and therefore even without the mortgage may not be able to afford the mortgage. Therefore, it is very important to assess the requirement for family protection above and beyond the mortgage cover.

This can come in a few forms such as level term lump sum, or an income monthly/annually for a duration [commonly until the youngest dependent is no longer dependent] and can also be index linked – IE linked to inflation so that the income received from the polices are not losing value year on year.

Typically, life insurance pay outs are not liable to income tax, but of course could be liable for inheritance tax if the estate is over a certain level. There are ways to negate this under the use of a trust, which is something you should discuss with your advisor as it is too complex to discuss within a book.

When we discuss life insurance protection with a property investor we are typically not looking at a policy per mortgage more one for the portfolio. Every investor's situation is going to be different.

So, advice in this area should be tailored not just to your current situation but also taking into account your future plans for borrowing. Having a strong business plan which outlines where you expect to take your borrowing and portfolio over the next 5 to 10 years is a good idea and this plan should be discussed with the broker giving the advice on your protection requirements.

It is common that we find a couple or partnership is lead by an alpha individual who is taking the full responsibility for the investing in property strategy. The partner is somewhat coming along for the ride, and whilst of course is active in decision making they would not want to do this by themselves. As such significantly planning needs to be considered around what happens should the alpha individual pass away.

It is common that we find a couple or partnership is lead by an alpha individual who is taking the full responsibility for the investing in property strategy. The partner is somewhat coming along for the ride, and whilst of course is active in decision making they would not want to do this by themselves. As such significantly planning needs to be considered around what happens should the alpha individual pass away.

Relevant life

As a property investor it might be appropriate to look at whether a policy via a limited company you own is viable to protect your portfolio and family. A relevant life policy is basically a death in service policy for an employee.

If you own an SPV property company and are a director of this company, you are in fact an employee and therefore can benefit from the tax advantages of having the company pay for the insurance policy for you. For higher rate tax payers the savings can be substantial. However, you do not need to be a higher rate tax payer to take out a policy.

Certain criteria will apply to the levels of cover you can take out. Most insurers will want to make sure the level of cover is relevant to the needs of the employee applying, and as such a limit of between, 25 and 30 times income is often placed on the policy. However, an explanation that you retain income within a company and have significant debt may allow an extension of the income multiples criteria.

Critical Illness cover
Like a life insurance policy and critical illness policy can be taken out to protect the mortgage on a decreasing term. They typically have a life insurance attached to them and will be a life or earlier critical illness policy.

It's really important to take advice on these types of policies and not just shop around on price. Every provider will have very different criteria and different critical illnesses covered, and different severities of the same critical illness. It can be a mine field and one we suggest you utilize a broker with good knowledge to help guide you through.

    Shopping for this policy on price leaves you at risk of buying a substandard policy for your requirements. The reason being is there is no manufacturing involved in insurance. The only way you can reduce the cots is reducing the risks, and therefore that means covering less.

    Some people have poor opinions of these types of policies because they've heard they don't pay out, when in fact they do, and the major insurers at a significantly high rate well in to the 90%s, but those that don't get a pay out will be for a couple of reasons. The policy criteria wasn't met, or the medical information submitted at application was inaccurate either by incompetence or intention- either way the policy was void.

Income protection policies

These policies may also be referred to as permanent health insurances. They are designed to replace you net income should you be off sick from work and your employer benefits have ceased. They are complex policies that need to be set up by an advisor to ensure that you have the correct advice on when the policy should start paying, and that you have protected the correct amount monthly.

These policies can pay out in different ways. Monthly until your retirement age should you be seriously or critically ill and unable to return to work indefinitely, all the way down to a limited pay out period of 2 years within a set defined period- typically until you retire.

These policies are under-utilised in the market, however, are some of the most important that should be considered by anyone taking out a mortgage, and to be fair anyone who has an income. Even if they are a tenant or living at home with parents. As an investor I would be suggesting all of my tenants had this type of policy in place to help protect my rent being paid in the event they fell ill and were unable to work.

These policies are complex. I will say it again. Take proper advice when setting them up.

Buildings and contents

All mortgage lenders will require the buildings to be adequately insured for at least the "rebuild" value supplied by the surveyor. This is the cost of rebuilding the entire property from the ground up.

These can vary massively from property to property. If you imagine rebuilding a mid-terrace for example, it is likely you will also need to rebuild, or at least do significant work to the adjoining properties both sides.

It is fair to say that the only compulsory insurance is Buildings. You can of course take this out whereever you wish as long as the insurance is adequate for the lenders purpose. They may charge an admin fee to confirm this, which is typically sub £50.

Contents insurance covers everything inside the property. A great analogy would be if you could pick the house up, turn it upside down- everything that falls out, including your carpets is contents.

It is really important to adequately insure you contents otherwise you may find you are under insured which ma result in an even lower pay out if the insurance company averages the claim. For example, if you insure yourself for £20,000 but on analysis of a full loss you were found to have £40,000 of contents, it is possible you will only receive a £10,000 pay out, as you were 50% insured.

17

Reviewing your insurances

Typically, insurances other than contents, which should be reviewed annually, would be review due to a life event. I think it's important to highlight what these life events are, but of course this is just a brief summary and is not exclusively when you should review the protection you have.

Adding to your portfolio

Whenever you purchase a new property you should analyse whether the insurances you have in place currently are adequate for the needs of your portfolio.

Many investors will of course take out larger policies than are initially needed to cover future expansion in the portfolio borrowing. It's still important however to look at your cover each and every time you amend your portfolio.

Moving house

This is the most common time people will review their insurances. Typically, because they have exposure to an advisor who will force the issue and engage the conversation.

This will usually be because debts are increasing and many of the other events have occurred whilst the client has been in ownership of their current home.

Career based

A change of job or pay change should trigger a review of your current protection. You should analyse whether you can now afford to cover things which were important which you could not budget for previously. An assessment of company benefits should also be undertaken. Has your sick pay arrangement changed? Do you now have a death in service policy?

Lots of things will change when your job changes or your career progresses even with the same company.

Marriage and Divorce

One of the first things that should be assessed at this point is whether your will is still as you wish it to be. Both marriage and divorce will have a potential impact on your requirements not only for income protection but life and critical illness cover.

It is possible that at this point you may need to consider the implication on someone else rather than just on yourself. This is where you should start to review family protection.

Children

Children are notoriously expensive. Forever. Just ask your parents, who may be gifting you a deposit to buy a house, and probably hoped that once you were out of school the costs would drop!

Ensuring the financial stability of your family is critically important for any parent, and it is your responsibility at this point to not only look at paying off any mortgage you have but ensuring that your children are financially supported until non-dependency – IE when they have their own income.

Family protection will be very important to be reviewed at this time and as such you should engage an advisor to discuss your situation, and priorities. Budgeting for an element of protection is critical and needs to be prioritised.

Wills & Trusts

It is important to have an up to date will to ensure that your wishes occur should the worst happen.

We say the worst, it is inevitable of course that we all die, and as such it will occur at some point. These are affordable and essential otherwise the government have already decided how your estate will be divided via the laws of intestacy.

Dying intestate means dying without a will, and the government have set standards of how and where your estate will be divided.

Whilst the use of a trust is a complex piece of advice, they should be considered for life insurance policies as they can help negate inheritance tax [under current legislation] and also speed up the funds getting to the intended recipient without the need for the policy to pass through a probate procedure, meaning the money is available instantly upon issue of a death certificate and can be utilised as you intended quickly.

This has excellent benefits of course with all considered. Most trusts set up for life insurance policies can be amended as life and time progresses to keep them up to date with your intention and wishes.

It is important to keep your will up to date and review whether any trust you have in place is still relevant to what you want to happen. All of the above life events should trigger a review not only of your protection policies, but also your estate planning and will.

Large portfolio landlords will have complex estates which could be subject to enormous rates of inheritance tax. It is really important to take proper estate planning advice from the very beginning of building your portfolio, and if you are reading this advice a bit too late for that, then this advice means this should be the very next thing that you do.

18
Types of adverse credit

Keeping your credit file in good order is an important factor when applying for a mortgage and ensuring you achieve the best interest rates available.

Adverse credit is a key factor in determining the interest rates that will be available to you, and if that adverse credit is too severe it is likely to cause a decline in your ability to borrow. This is especially true the smaller percentage deposit you have available.

In this section we will run through the types of adverse credit, and their potential impact on your ability to borrow. As a first time buyer we will assume you have a lower percentage deposit, and as such it is fair to say that any of the listed credit misdemeanors are likely to be a hindrance to acquiring lending.

Bankruptcy

If you are currently bankrupt, you are unable to borrow. Most lenders would require your bankruptcy to be 5 or 6 years behind you, whilst some will state they will not lend should you ever have been made bankrupt. This is about as serious as adverse credit can get.

IVA

An individual voluntary arrangement or IVA is often an alternative to bankruptcy. A deal with your creditors will be reached, and a set timescale set out with monthly payments.

Whilst in the IVA, it will be difficult to acquire further new lending.

Defaults

A default is a term used for when you have defaulted on the payments agreed on the credit contract. This is often registered following several missed payments.

CCJ

A county court judgement is often sort to enforce you to repay a debt, and the courts often agree a payment plan as part of it. Many defaults end up in subsequent CCJs.

Missed or late payments

A late payment or a missed payment on a credit agreement will also be registered as adverse credit. This may be on a loan, credit card or hire purchase, but can equally be relating to mobile telecommunications payments, utility bills [Gas, water and electricity] or any other monthly paid by a credit agreement set up.

Multiple of these types of missed payments will lead to a potential default or CCJ. These are deemed worse that missed or late payments.

Most lenders as we have already mentioned will expect to see a clean credit file. However, minor "blips" that are historic should not be an issue for most experienced brokers. More serious adverse credit will of course pose larger challenges.

It is important to obtain your credit file and monitor it continuously in our opinion. You should definitely provide your broker with a copy as early in the process as possible. This is important even if you don't have any adverse credit. This will allow them to accurately record payments and balances for any credit you have, but also see how the scoring systems are viewing you. It could be you have no credit, and as a young first time buyer this can also be a challenge as you have no history.

19
Improving your credit file

Some key things you can do to improve your credit file are quite simple to achieve, but please note whilst some will have an impact immediately credit files typically require time to improve and won't happen overnight.

Other than the obvious thing of paying the debts you have on time below are some fundamental things you can do to improve your credit score.

Register to vote

Being on the electoral roll is a way that you can be electronically identified as resident at a particular address. Being registered carries points towards your score, so unless there is a particular reason to not be registered- make sure you are.

Have some active credit

Having a mobile phone contract and a credit card with a low limit that is used and paid off monthly is a great way to demonstrate credit worthiness and build your score. However, ensure that anything you take out is set up to be paid on a direct debit and that the payments are made on time. Too frequently people forget to make payments when they are required to be done manually, and this will cripple your efforts to improve your credit score and have the completely opposite effect of what you are trying to achieve.

Reduce available credit

If you already have lots of credit cards, whether they have credit balances or not it is best to reduce these down. This happens a lot when people balance transfer by opening a new card facility and do not close the facility that they have transferred from. Over time large available credit facilities are created, and this can actually reduce your score, and make lenders nervous.

Try not to move around a lot

We don't mean sit still! However, having lots of addresses in a short period of time will reduce your credit score. The score improves with consistency, and therefore ensuring that you have as few addresses over the last 3 years as possible is ideal for improving your score. Whilst multiple addresses will not automatically mean a decline, it is a factor when determining your credit score.

Keep your bank accounts in good order

Your current account activity will be a factor of your credit scoring, so staying in credit, or at worst within an agreed overdraft limit is critical. A healthy flow of cash through the account that ends in a net

positive gain each month will benefit your credit file.

Your current account activity will be a factor of your credit scoring, so staying in credit, or at worst within an agreed overdraft limit is critical. A healthy flow of cash through the account that ends in a net positive gain each month will benefit your credit file.

Each and every lender will have their own internal scoring system we have seen people with perfect scores on Experian or Equifax be declined by a lender because their available credit was too high across their credit cards based on their earned income.

20
Common Investor Mistakes

Many property courses will teach you to use your credit cards to fund your purchases. Possibly buying something outright if you can raise enough across multiple cards, but also to be utilised as a deposit. In the deposits chapter I cover why this cannot be done.

Many property courses also suggest using your credit cards for the refurbs on properties and getting multiple cards with very high limits, accepting all limit increases and for want of a better phrase, racking up enormous unsecured credit card debt in the pursuit of financial freedom from property. Using debt to create cashflow is not necessarily a bad strategy in business.

Most very successful businesses will do this. However, when you constantly need to raise finance and it is a personal credit file that will be checked, this strategy should be used with extreme caution as there is no limited protection for you like big businesses have, and defaulting on large debts could risk other assets you hold.

This is an enormous mistake for many investors. The more unsecured debt you have the worse your credit score will be. Even lenders who do not credit score, and only credit check or profile will become exceptionally nervous of lending to anyone with enormous debt to income ratios. Whilst it is not a problem to have some credit card debt, and a couple of credit cards, it is never advised to take out enormous levels of debt on these cards on the basis you hope to be able to remortgage out of the debt in the future.

What you may find is your application is declined, and you are stuck with high interest debt on credit cards, which you cannot afford to pay, and that can then be game over.

Another key mistake we see investors making is trying to do too much too soon. Lenders like to see steady progression and not zero to £Xm in lending in a few months, without adequate financial backing for such an increase.

Many lenders will look at how many properties you have purchased and the experience you have and have been known to decline an application and say they will reconsider in 1 year time once the properties have been let and a history of how the applicant is dealing with the new debt and responsibility has been established. This isn't to say you cannot buy property quickly and grow your portfolio, you just need to be in a stable financial position to do so otherwise you will hit some road blocks which will slow you up.

Finally, too frequently we see property investor who take a very laidback approach to actually paying their bills. Not necessarily the finance costs, like credit cards or mortgages, but things like utility bills and mobile phones. These are common missed, late or irregular payments on credit files because they haven't been set up as DDs. They will show as such on your credit file and will cause significant issues obtaining finance when there is a pattern of poor financial management.

When you are looking at one of your biggest ongoing costs being that of finance interest rates, it should be of upmost importance to be on top of the management of your credit file.

All payments should be made on time, no matter how big or small they are and direct debits for minimum payments should be set up in all circumstances to insure no late or missed payments.

Active management of your bank accounts, including ensuring the balances are available to pay your committed expenditure is essential to achieving the lowest rates in the market. Where possible keeping the bank account in credit and not using overdrafts is also very preferable.

It will of course be possible to in most cases achieve some form of lending if a 25% deposit is available. But you will likely be looking at significant interest rate differences if your credit file is a mess.

21
Bridging Finance

Bridging finance is a very popular, and useful source of finance for the property developer and buy to let investor. A much more flexible source of financing it offers opportunities where traditional term products do not. In this section I'll run through how bridging finance works, the different types of bridging finance, the benefits and the possible pitfalls of it.

There are 2 types of bridging finance. Open and closed bridging.

Open bridging will not have an end date and will just keep running until it is settled. This is not a very common form of finance. These will typically be more expensive than closed bridging as they offer more flexibility to the borrower.

Closed bridging is for a set duration, typically somewhere between 6 and 24 months, dependent of the project requirements. A strategy to pay the bridging loan off at the end of the term must be in place prior to the bridge being taken out and will be a fundamental part of the underwriting.

Bridging typically is either a first or second charge on a property, and sometimes a blend of both, taking first charge on a purchase property and second on an already owned and financed asset with equity. This presents potential as if the combined available equity across the purchase property and already owned property is enough you are able to raise effectively 100% of the purchase price on a bridge by utilising the available equity.

Most bridging lenders will consider a loan to value up to 85% depending on the project and your current experience level.

Monthly interest is typically charged, at rates that are set for individual projects and based on the risk to the lender of the project and the individuals applying. Your track record is very important and the more experienced you become with using bridging for development the better rates you can expect to achieve.

Interest can be charged in a few ways.

Monthly interest only payments can be charged. Similar to a buy to let mortgage, with payments set put at the start of the agreement.

Rolled up or deferred interest. You make not monthly payments and interest is added to the loan each month and compounded. You pay it all when the loan is settled at the end of the term.

Retained interest. When the interest for the whole term is retained from the initial advance, and when you settle the advance at the end of the term any unused interest is rebated to you.

Typically, a bridging loan will have no early repayment penalties for settlement at any point after the first month.

Refurb Bridge to Let products

Some bridging and buy to let lenders have launched very useful bridge to let products for properties which are currently not in a lettable condition, but which you intend to let moving forward.

The product would release the bridge funds initially, and value the property in its current state and once the work is done as a guaranteed value projection. This is useful as you know your done up value, and as long as proposed works are completed satisfactorily and the reinspection confirms this you will then move on to a term buy to let product without further underwriting, and potentially within a couple of months of the purchase avoiding the need to wait 6 months to remortgage due to money laundering regulations.

When the bridge converts to the term buy to let product the loan to value will be of the new value and capital raised will be released back to the borrower. Many investors are using this type of product to buy, refurbish, let and grow a very profitable portfolio within only a low initial input of funds.

Using a Bridging product for 100% Finance

It is very possible depending on the equity you have in your properties for you to raise 100% finance for your purchase, and potentially also your refurbishment costs. The key to this is equity available.

When a second charge is involved – IE a bridge on a property that is already mortgaged, typically the loan to value across all security cannot exceed 70%. So, utilising this knowledge you can possibly therefore use property you already own, maybe your own home, as security for your investments.

Let's look at some maths:

- Own home worth £325,000
- Current high street mortgage £190,000
- New Buy to let purchase £80,000
- 70% of £325,000 is £227,500 - £190,000 = £37,500 can be use from your own home
- 70% of the purchase price at £80,000 is £56,000 + £37,500 = gross loan of £93,500 meaning we could achieve a net loan [net of interest retained and fees] of our purchase price of £80,000.

This would be a risky strategy if you were unable to significantly improve the property to at least a value of £125,000 within a 12 month period.

This is the value you would need to be able to remortgage the debt of £93,500 away from the bridging lender at a 75% LTV.

Of course, a sales exit may also be viable, if you could achieve a significant increase in the value. Therefore, the bridge across 2 properties could be utilised as a mechanism for flipping properties without having to put in a deposit.

Overtime this would allow you to build up a capital base which could of course be used to reduce finance rates as deposits are increased or do more properties simultaneously to grow quicker.

Bridging can be a very useful tool for the property investor, but in comparison to term products it is of course priced based on convenience and risk. The risks are higher both for the lender and the borrower as there needs to be a certain level of improvement in most cases for there to be a viable exit.

As with any financial commitment time and advice should be taken to ensure this is the right approach for you and that you are fully aware of the risks involved in entering in to such short term deals.

An added risk which has not been talked about much recently as the property market has been on an upward curve, is the risk that property prices fall, quite dramatically so, and any improvements you make will not stack up to your done-up value projections.

This is becoming more and more common as down valuations on projected values are being seen in the market place due to fall in demand and rise in available stock.

The lack of comparable evidence available to surveyors is also a key factor in the trend towards lowering values as they have no evidence to back up the numbers they are presented with so cautiously value the property to protect their own reputations and liability insurances against potentially being off the mark with their personal opinions and assessments.

22

Flipping Profit

There are many ways in which this strategy can be undertaken. In this chapter I will run through the most common I have seen successfully undertaken. It is important to say that when you are flipping properties. Or more accurately, buying them with the sole purpose of improving them to sell on for a profit, it is likely that the tax implications on the transaction will be different to that of a transaction where your intention was to purchase, hold and rent the property and then sold the property for a profit. Our advice is always to consult with a personal and property tax specialist prior to engaging in any transaction so as not to be caught out on the backend with a large unexpected tax bill. [That is not to say a tax bill will not be large- you'll just be expecting it]

Flipping with bridging

The most obvious financing strategy would be to flip a property utilising bridging finance. This is short term lending ideal for this. You could choose whether to make monthly interest payments or retain the interest from the start. You will of course need to ensure you allow enough time to refurb the property, market and sell the property through to completion.

The bridging product will likely come with penalties attached if you do not repay the loan by the end of the specified period you took it out for, and as such it is usually advised to be very cautious and take a slightly longer term of 12 months + to allow for enough time to complete the project. Of course, you will want to assess the cost differences of committing to a longer term.

Of course, you can utilise the potential of 100% lending using bridging finance to borrow the costs of acquisition with the possibility of financing the refurb costs if of course there is enough equity is available to be put forward as security.

A second strategy is to buy a property as your main residential home on a term residential product. This will only work as a strategy for properties that would be classed as habitable. You will of course also need to be able to live in the property whilst the work is being conducted, but this strategy can work well for those who are maybe able to reside in an "under construction" environment.

I have seen this strategy work very well for single individuals who have the skill sets to do the majority of the refurbishment work themselves or have affordable access to trades through their networks of friends and colleagues to get the work done. It's important to stress if you are looking at short term finance and won't sell and buy by porting a residential mortgage across but instead wish to sell, and not retain the mortgage then residential term finance is not suitable.

One particular client sticks in my mind who over a period of time bought, lived in, and refurbished several properties. Only ever owning one property at a time and porting his residential mortgage across tying in a sale and purchase. Over time this client built up more and more equity to the point that they did not actually need a mortgage to purchase the types of property they wanted to live in and develop and were making a profit from each flipped property.

They were very successful with this strategy, but it has to be said did live in a development site for most of their lives whilst doing this.

It is important that you take proper tax advice on the above strategy.

Important things to remember:

You need to be very much in to the details with the costings. The money can be made in the purchasing and not necessarily the selling when it comes to flipping properties. Negotiating on the right property and achieving the right price will dictate your success with flipping properties.

Secondly, and just as importantly getting really good and accurate quotes from trades prior to purchase will ensure you don't end up buying for £100,000, spending £40,000 and ending up with a property valued at £125,000.

Building a local team of reliable trades you work with regularly, can trust and know that they come in on price at a high quality is very important.

THE PROPERTY INVESTOR'S FINANCE MANIFESTO

GLOSSARY of Terms

AIP – Agreement in principal.

BTL – Buy to Let

DIP – Decision in principal

An initial credit check by a lender to establish whether they will consider your full application or not.

FMA – Full mortgage application
The point at which you apply for your mortgage against a specific property

HMO – House of Multiple Occupancy

HMRC – Her Majesties Revenue & Customs

RICS – Royal institute of chartered surveyors

SDLT – Stamp duty Land Tax

Notes section:

MICHAEL WEBB

Printed in Great Britain
by Amazon